The Complete Guide to Palmistry

Batia Shorek

The ancient subject of palmistry includes the characteristics of the fingers and palm, the structure of the mounds, analysis of lines, and the meaning of signs.

The hand is the human organ that comes into contact with the material world, and reflects the psychological properties of the individual. The mounds, lines and signs of the palm provide us with extensive information about the individual. The palm can become a map for understanding the individual.

The structure of the palm and the fingers is invariable, as is the structure of the mounds. The lines and signs, however, change constantly. Thus the palm relates both to the inherited aspects of the individual and to his or her dynamic and changing features.

This book discusses the basic theories of palmistry according to the classic approach in a clear and easily understandable manner. The Complete Guide to Palmistry includes a large number of illustrations and pictures that make it easy to grasp and learn the material.

Batia Shorek (age 50) was exposed to the subject of palmistry in her parents' home, and began to work in the field on a professional basis while studying at university. Batia offers courses and gives lectures on various aspects of mystics, and has written books and articles in professional journals. Batia Shorek lives in Israel with her husband and their two children.

The Complete Guide to
Palmistry

Batia Shorek

Astrolog Publishing House

Astrolog Publishing House
P.O.Box 1123, Hod Hasharon 45111, Israel
TEL/FAX. 972-9-7412044
E-Mail: info@astrolog.co.il
Astrolog Web Site: www.astrolog.co.il

© Batia Shorek 1998

ISBN 965-494-009-4

Published by Astrolog Publishing House 1998

Distribution:
U.S.A & CANADA by APG - associated publishers group
U.K & EUROPE by DEEP BOOKS
EAST ASIA by CKK Ltd

Printed in Israel
10   9   8   7   6   5   4   3   2   1

TABLE OF CONTENTS

THE HAND

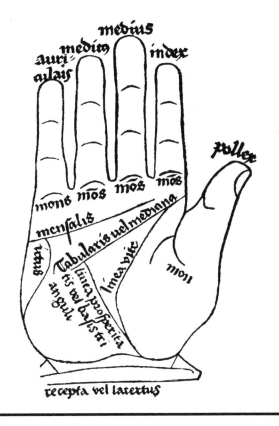

Why the Hand?

The linguistic definition of the hand is really quite simple — it is the part of the body found at the end of the arm, which is used for holding and touching. But the hand is really so much more than that. It is the part of our body through which we come in contact with the material world.

The hands are not just another pair of extremities that cannot be used for walking: they can grasp objects, and because of the structure of the opposing thumb, our hands become much more important than merely another pair of appendages.

There are philosophers who claim that the development of the human hand is, in essence, the development of civilization. Prehistoric man, resembling the monkey, could hold only stones and branches in his hand; over time, numerous tools and devices were developed and man's hands were able to use them.

If we compare the palm of the hand with the sole of the foot we can see immediately how appropriate the tools and devices, with which we come into daily contact, are to the palm of the hand.

Of all the parts of the hand, it is the thumb which stands out in importance. The muscular flexibility of the thumb and its unique structure opposing the other fingers is what differentiates, according to many, between man and the ape (anatomically speaking).

The hand is important not only as an anatomic expression of man, but also as a psychological expression. There are nervous hands, sensitive hands, lazy hands, "left" hands, as we commonly endow hands with characteristic traits. No one speaks of lazy thighs, or nervous ears, but a person's hands reflect his character, and therefore they reflect the same characteristics and talents as the person to whom they belong.

One of the most interesting things about the hand is the way the skin changes. The skin at the tip of the fingers, for example, is quite sensitive (second in sensitivity only to the skin on the lips). The palm is more sensitive than the back of the hand, while the skin on the outside of the fingers is quite tough. Sensitivity is determined by the number of nerve endings found beneath the surface of the skin, and the way in which the nerve endings are distributed in the palm of the hand is both anatomically and psychologically significant.

The hand is a sophisticated tool for touching and feeling, and its sensitivity can sometimes reach incredible levels, such is with the hands of a blind person or other people whose sense of touch has developed more than their other senses.

The lines on the palm are constantly changing, but similar rules govern all the lines. The structure of the line of life, for example, is influenced by muscular changes at the base of the thumb; the line of heart is affected by the muscles which close the palm; the line of intellect is influenced by the contrast between the hand and the fingers, and so on. The fact that these lines get their shape from and can be changed by the muscles as they react to a person's activities, needs, and impulses is what gives these lines their significance.

The surface of the skin is like a sensitive record which absorbs and holds a person's needs and impulses, and reveals them to the palmist who possesses the knowledge to interpret what is written there. Therefore, despite many varied attempts at reading a person's character using other parts of the body, it is palmistry that has been most successful and has gained the most followers.

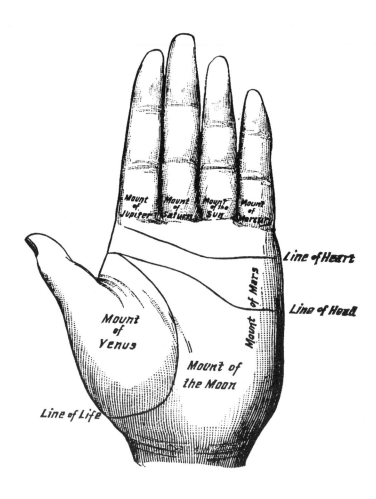

The Palm as a map for understanding the individual.

Techniques of Palmistry

Palmistry can be performed anywhere — in a crowd or in a room with only the palmist and the client, during the day or at night. Professional palmists make sure there is a suitable setting — a room in which the client feels comfortable, yet also senses a certain air of mystery. But this kind of environment is only necessary for someone who wants to make palm reading his profession.

A bit of advice will not hurt the amateur palmist either:

It is best to read someone's palm when you are alone with him or her. That way, you can concentrate on his palm without any extraneous distractions.

The client must be seated facing the palmist, about a hand's length away. There should be strong, natural light on the palms of the hands, or a light with a lamp shade that can concentrate the light on the palms, without blinding the reader or the client.

A magnifying glass would be helpful in diagnosing marks that may be found on the palm.

It is best to prepare diagrams of the palm upon which the palmist can indicate the lines and marks found on the client's hands. (This makes it easier to compare the right hand with the left hand, and to identify changes that take place over time.)

It is also a good idea for the amateur palmist to keep an illustration of the palm handy, which indicates the location of mounts and lines on the hand.

Regarding the actual reading of the palm, remember that one should work from the general to the more detailed — from a general impression of the palm, to the fingers, to the thumb, and on to the mounts, lines, and marks. Do not attempt to take shortcuts. Do not go into details before you have a general perception.

The first attempt will be difficult, and perhaps even confusing. But with time, and with the experience and knowledge gained, you will learn to read palms and to know others, as well as yourself, through the palms of their hands.

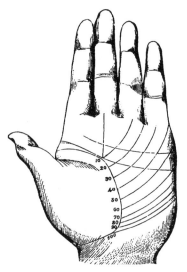

The periods of life in the hand.

Chirognomy and Chiromancy

Although palmistry is considered to be a single subject, we can really define two main branches:

1. **Chirognomy**. The branch of palmistry dealing with the shape of the hand — the palm, the back of the hand, the fingers, and the proportions between the different parts of the hand.

2. **Chiromancy**. The branch of palmistry dealing with the lines, mounts, and other marks found on the palm.

The palmist, after having determined his general impression, begins with chirognomy and ends with chiromancy, that is, he goes from the general to the detailed.

The General Impression

Palmists begin their inspection with a general examination and then go on to look at the smaller details of the palm. From chirognomy (shape of the hand and fingers) to chiromancy (lines and marks on the palm). However, before beginning with the chirognomy, the palmist must possess a general impression of the client's hand.

Taking into account the external appearance of the client, his clothing, and the way he walks, the palmist will attempt to discover small details about the person standing before him. These details can help provide a general direction, but they must not be used to determine the client's character, and certainly not to foretell his future.

Details that cannot be reinforced by the lines of a person's palm should be disregarded!

Therefore, the palmist must be cautioned against first impressions gathered from the client's appearance, and should direct his attention to the first impression he gets from the client's hands. This will put him on surer ground.

There are seven stages to this first impression, and they should be gone through stage by stage — in a quick but not rash manner. These stages will guide us from a general impression to a closer examination of details.

General Appearance of the Hands:

1. Position and Movement

When taking a general view of the hands, we must pay attention to two things: the position of the hands and the movement of the hands. It is best to assess these details before the client seats himself.

The position of the hands is assessed on the basis of:

1. Hands that are held behind the back indicate an elemental nature, and a tendency to examine and plan every activity. (This position is characteristic of members of the military, for example, or engineers.)

2. Hands that are held in front of the body indicate self-respect and appreciation, and the tendency to act carefully and cautiously.

3. Hands that are held at one's side signify a lack of self-confidence.

. 4. Hands that are held so that the left hand is at the side and the arm of the right hand is bent across the chest, suggest a tendency towards an exaggerated sense of self-importance and an attempt to hide a lack of self-reliance. (Note: for left-handed people, the right hand will be by their side and the left hand will be bent across the chest.)

When studying **the movements of the hands** we differentiate between sharp, short, and rapid movements that indicate nervousness, and between long, deliberate, slow movements, which indicate peace and inner tranquillity.

(Palmists should be careful not to attribute too much to the movements of the hands, and in a case where there is a contradiction between what is seen from the palm and what you might learn from the movements of the hands, the palm should take precedence over the movements.)

2. Sweat on the Palm

We differentiate between a sweaty palm and a dry palm:

1. A sweaty palm indicates nervousness and lack of self-confidence.

2. A dry palm means a sense of self-confidence and openness towards others.

3. Hair on the Back of the Hand

The hair found on the back of the hand should be checked by examining the amount of hair, the type of hair, and its color. We must look at the details separately and remember that the degree of hairiness is determined by the number of hairs, not by their color or coarseness.

1. If the back of the hand is hairy, it indicates strong desires and a warm temperament. People with this kind of hand are energetic, particularly in their sexual activities.

2. If the back of the hand has little or no hair, this shows a calm nature with a tendency to do things in moderation.

The hairs are divided on the basis of their coarseness and color into two main groups:

1. Hairs that are thin and delicate, which are usually light colored, indicate a passive, stable nature, with a tendency towards submissiveness.

2. Hairs that are thick and coarse, which are usually dark colored (from black to red) signify an active, although unstable, nature and a tendency towards quick mood changes.

(Despite the fact that there are those who emphasize examining the hair on men's hands, we must remember that such an examination is no less important for women. We may find, for example, that a women's hand that has dark and coarse hair clearly indicates intense and passionate sexual activity.)

4. The Network of Lines on the Palm

The network of lines on the palm refers to the number of lines that can be seen when first looking at the palm:

1. An abundance of lines indicates a nervous, sensitive nature, someone who "takes everything to heart."

Numerous lines on a soft hand indicates a tendency towards hypochondria.

Numerous lines on a rough hand signifies a tendency towards social action and doing for others.

2. A small number of lines suggests a calm nature, that does not worry, and even a tendency towards indifference. This type of person often lacks sensitivity.

5. The Color of the Hand

The color of the hand lends additional signs for learning about a person. Each palm has its own particular coloring, and these may be classified as follows (in comparison with the color of the skin):

1. A whitish, pale coloring indicates poor health, a lack of energy, and a tendency to tire quickly. The person shows signs of selfishness and does not form honest relationships.

2. A yellowish coloring signifies spiritual depression. Such a person displays suspicion and bitterness towards those around him and tends towards angry outbursts.

3. A pink or reddish coloring indicates good health and lots of energy. This person loves life, is happy and hopeful, and enjoys warm and passionate relationships with those around him.

6. The Skin on the Hand

We differentiate between smooth, soft skin and between coarse, rough skin (we must be careful and not interpret blisters or calluses due to hard work as rough skin). We must always attempt to find the skin's basic characteristics, and this can be accomplished by examining the skin between the fingers and below the Mount of Venus.

1. Soft, smooth skin indicates a youthful spirit no matter what the client's age. People with smooth, soft skin will keep their childlike spirit even into old age.

2. Rough, scaly skin indicates that they have lost their youthful spirit at a relatively young age.

7. The Way the Palm Feels

We can examine the way the palm feels by pressing with the thumb on the Mount of Venus, and we may differentiate between a firm palm or a soft palm. For a soft palm we also examine the palm's flexibility, by evaluating the resilience of the Mount of Venus.

1. A soft and flexible palm indicates a soft character and lack of self-confidence.

A soft and stable palm communicates proper spiritual balance and a peaceful character.

2. A firm palm shows an abundance of energy and striving for accomplishment.

But when the palm is stiff and lacks flexibility, this indicates aspiration towards short-term achievement and a lack of planning long-ranging steps.

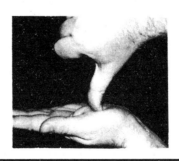

The Size of the Hands

We can differentiate between large hands and small hands.

1. People with large hands enjoy taking care of details and for the most part, tend to deal in jobs involving accuracy; the handwriting of those with large hands is often small.

2. People with small hands like to plan and deal with big things, primarily in the area of administration; they work in areas requiring generalizations and their handwriting is usually large and energetic.

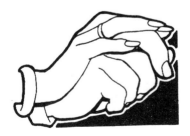

The Size of the Palm

The size of the palm is defined in comparison with the size of the entire hand and the length of the fingers. We tend to speak of five types:

1. A large, wide hand communicates good health, sexuality, and energetic mental and physical activity.

2. A large, narrow hand signifies a spontaneous nature, a tendency towards intellectual rather than physical activity, a tendency to worry about everything, and to a certain extent also signifies a person pursued by unfounded fears.

3. A medium-sized hand shows spiritual balance and good health, proper judgment and a tendency to study things.

4. A small hand, particularly if it is soft, indicates a love of luxuries, and a certain degree of laziness.

5. A "giant" hand, which is disproportionally large, signifies a tendency towards violence — an unstable person who may be dangerous to himself and to others.

Right and Left

A palmist must read both the left and the right palms. Just a bit of experience will reveal to the palmist that a person's two palms, in terms of lines and other marks, do not resemble one another. Quite the contrary, the differences between one palm and the other are truly remarkable.

The left palm, whose lines are determined at birth, shows the person's character and what he has inherited from his parents. It is clear that the palmist cannot foretell the future from this palm.

The right palm, which is primarily read for the purpose of foretelling the future, teaches us about the person's learned abilities, the possibilities hidden within him, the factors that have influenced his past and that will affect his future. This is the palm whose lines change as the person changes, and which indicate in what direction he will turn. Studying this palm will verify what is seen in the left palm, and displays the developments and transformations that have taken place in the past, signs of which can also be seen in the left palm.

There are those who say that the left hand is determined by fate, while the right hand is determined by a person's will.

The palmist will hold both palms, examining one in comparison with the other. This examination will show one important thing — the degree of change that has taken place, or will take place, in the person's life.

If the lines on the left palm and the right palm are very different from each other, this indicates an inconsistent lifestyle, a tendency to do a variety of things, as well as a tendency towards adventurousness and openness. If the lines of the two hands are similar to each other, this shows a consistent lifestyle, one that is stable and unchanging.

The palmist begins by reading the left palm, from which he will learn about the persons basic characteristics and talents (inherited), and will then go on to the right hand, from which he will learn about what has taken place in the person's past and what his future holds. In the event the client is left-handed, the order of the process is, of course, reversed.

There is a special problem when dealing with left-handed clients. In most cases, their right hands indicate their character and their left hand indicates their future (when a person is left-handed from birth). However, there are cases when a person is left-handed, but their palms resemble those of a person whose right hand is dominant. Experience will teach the palmist to immediately distinguish these exceptions.

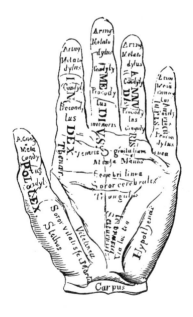

The Shape of the Hand

If we understand the harmony that exists between the palm and the fingers, the shape of the hand teaches us about the person's spiritual and physical balance.

The palm represents the person's fundamental characteristics — intellect, the factors shaping his values; character; and physical and spiritual health.

The fingers represent the way in which a person expresses his characteristics: his temperament, energy, and his softness or coarseness.

Only rarely are the hands in perfect harmony. More often, there is a certain amount of disagreement between the palm and the fingers.

We can divide the different types of hands into basic groups and can find the characteristics for each group.

The most recognized differentiation is that devised by Captain Stanislas d'Arpentigny, which was also used by Count Haumon (who was known as "Cheiro"), which divides the hands into seven main types.

1. **The Elemental Hand**. Large palm, short thumb, and short, thick fingers. Tendency towards physical activity and an aversion to any activity requiring thought.

The elemental hand is described as "quite broad, quite thick, quite firm." For the most part, the nails are short and wide and the palm is the most distinctive feature of the entire hand.

People with this type of hand lack imagination and are lazy and apathetic; the palm is covered by a weak network of lines. People with this type of palm tend to enjoy simple pleasures, are unable to control their passions, and are not interested in art or literature.

The short, thick thumb is close to the hand, indicating a tendency towards verbal aggressiveness, and an almost total lack of ambition.

2. **The Spatulate Hand**. The palm is of moderate size and the fingers are strong and developed, showing a tendency towards practicality, moderation, and self-control.

The spatulate hand characterizes methodical people who think in an orderly fashion. They are useful, law-abiding citizens with regular habits. The spiritual and physical worlds are limited to defined areas, which are also, usually, limited.

There are those who describe the spatulate hand as the hand of someone who is a "slave to a particular subject, idea or job." The large, developed thumb indicates that the person with the spatulate hand has "both feet on the ground" but "cannot see what is on the surface."

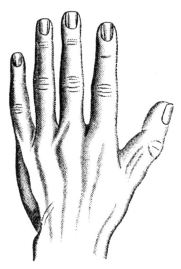

With the spatulate hand, which is quite common, the fingers significant effect the person's character:

Short, thick fingers (on the spatulate hand) — greed, narrow horizons, and activity primarily in the commercial sphere;

Long, thick fingers — mental ability and a tendency towards scientific research, primarily in the area of the natural sciences;

Flat fingers — a tendency towards creativity and action in daily life (but not in an artistic sense);

Conical fingers — a tendency towards spiritual activity and spiritual creativity (which results, therefore, in an internal struggle between the methodical practicality which is expressed by the palm, and the spiritual creativity denoted by the fingers). Activity in the area of the arts, letters, and music;

Fingers that are shaped differently (in the spatulate hand) indicate a tendency towards moodiness and a lack of perseverance which is in contrast to the basic tendency of people with spatulate hands;

Fingers with prominent joints (in a spatulate hand) show attention to detail in any field the person undertakes.

3. **The Philosophic Hand**. A long palm, large thumb, and long fingers with prominent joints, indicate a tendency towards logic and intellect and an escape from blind faith and idealism.

The philosophic hand characterizes people who love wisdom, people with "an intuitive talent to find the right path." People with this type of hand deal primarily in the natural and social sciences; the large thumb with phalanges that are identical in length demonstrate a tendency to examine and investigate those subjects that interest them.

With this type of palm, the fingers are long with prominent joints and long fingernails, indicating patience and attention to small details. People with the philosophic hand tend, on occasion, to display external signs of being out of the ordinary, but essentially, they are not extraordinary.

4. **The Practical Hand**. A square or triangular-shaped hand with fingers that appear more flat than round communicates a tendency towards optimism, self-confidence, energy, and ambition.

The practical hand is characterized by a large thumb. The phalange with the fingernail appears flat. The practical hand is characteristic of "working people," "business people," and "people whose lives are controlled by accounts and balance sheets." Work is of the utmost importance to people with this type of hand.

The most noticeable characteristic of people with a practical hand is the striving towards independence and personal freedom. People with this type of hand have a strong degree of mobility; they are the ones who build the social foundations, they are the ones who settle in new areas, they are the seafarers and the discoverers of new worlds. They stubbornly persevere towards the achievement of their goals, even at the cost of personal sacrifice.

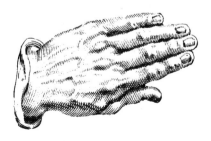

5. **The Artistic Hand**. A long, medium-sized hand, long thumb, with long, conical fingers indicates a tendency towards creativity and openness, particular in the artistic sphere.

This type of hand can be recognized by the fact that despite the palm being medium-sized, the fingers are long and the phalange with the fingernail (as well as the fingernail itself) tends to be round; typical characteristics of people with an artistic hand are drive and desire, in varying degrees.

We may distinguish between different types of thumbs on an artistic hand:

1. A small thumb with a medium palm is the hand of the artist, the lover of beauty.

2. A large thumb with a relatively large palm is the hand of a person who deals in art, who uses art to achieve his economic goals.

3. A large thumb with a very large palm is the hand of an artist who is controlled by his desires.

The artistic hand immediately portrays the person's artistic and creative tendencies, but only after examining the entire hand can we know how this tendency is actually expressed.

6. **The Psychic Hand**. A small, long, and narrow palm with long, slender fingers indicates a tendency towards fantasy, towards a love of beauty, and to escape from material reality to the world of imagination.

This lovely hand is pleasant to the touch; the fingers are tapered and the thumb is small and flexible, with the phalange of the fingernail being relatively long.

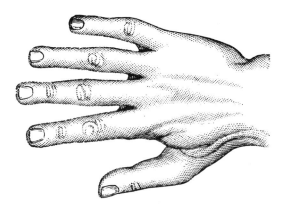

People with this type of hand are blessed with rare intellectual characteristics, but they are controlled by their idealism, so they often find themselves as outsiders and isolated from society as a result. They lack a sense of reality and are unstable; often, they live their lives in the shadow of some "patron" or family member who takes care of their material needs and helps "to keep their feet firmly on the ground."

7. **The Mixed Hand**. With fingers that are clearly different from one another, this type of hand is difficult to characterize and thus difficult to read. People with this type of hand tend towards variety, and sometimes the different paths in their lives become confused and oppose each other. These are people with a good ability to adapt and they are pleasant social beings who are liked by those around them.

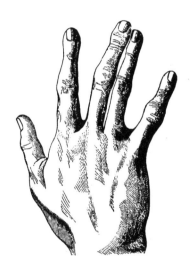

The Fingers

The fingers should be examined from several aspects: the shape of the fingers; the length of the fingers in comparison with each other; the phalanges; and joints of the fingers. The thumb and fingernails should receive special attention.

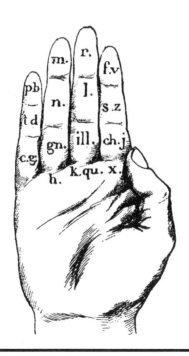

The Shape of the Fingers

The basic distinction is that between long fingers and short fingers (in relationship to the length of the palm):

Long fingers indicate a tendency towards precision, accuracy, and attention to details.

Short fingers indicate impulsiveness, quick thinking, and intuitiveness.

Fingers that are long, broad, and solid indicate spiritual balance, aggressive nature, and intellectual ability.

Fingers that are long and narrow signify sensitivity, good taste, and a tendency towards minute details. These are characteristic of philosophers and diplomats.

Long, flat fingers communicate a tendency towards a suspicious nature, indifference to others, and a developed sense of criticism that can be "poisonous."

Medium fingers (neither long or short in relation to the size of the palm) that are well-formed indicate bright thinking and firm control of any sphere in which the person deals.

Short, clumsy fingers suggest an impulsive nature, lack of consideration, lack of stability, and a stubborn character.

Fingers that are short and very clumsy signify cruelty and stubbornness.

 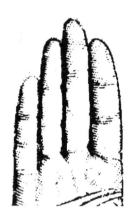

Short, square-shaped fingers show healthy logic, feelings of faithfulness, and an ability to adapt.

Fingers that are short and conical (round, larger at the base than at the top), indicate an imagination which tends towards fabricating lies and selfishness.

Meaty fingers that are thick at the bottom suggest excessive selfishness and a lack of consideration for others. This is a person that cannot be trusted.

Slender fingers that have a tendency to bend backwards

hint at altruism, openness, and generosity, but also a weak will.

Solid, inflexible fingers indicate a person who knows exactly what he wants to achieve.

Thin fingers that have a tendency to bend inwards imply instability and a lack of courage.

Firm fingers (in contrast with solid fingers) that are not flexible indicate a lack of spiritual flexibility, ego, and slyness bordering on evil.

Fingers that are thick, short, and conical indicate selfishness and a love of extravagance, primarily with relation to the body.

Square-shaped fingers

Flat fingers

It is important to examine the length of the fingers with relation to one another:

If the first finger (closest to the thumb) is longer relative to the other fingers, this indicates a love for control and pride.

If the third finger (closest to the pinkie) is equal in length to the first finger, this shows a desire for fame and honor; if the third finger is longer than the first finger, this suggests a tendency toward gambling in all areas of life.

The pinkie should be examined in relation to the thumb. The more the pinkie is shaped like the thumb, the more harmony there will be in the person's nature.

Conical fingers

Sharp, round fingers

The Phalanges

The first phalange (with the fingernail) indicates the intellectual abilities of the person being examined. The longer the phalange, the stronger the tendency is towards mental activity, primarily when the end of the finger is round. When the first phalange is flat, this shows a tendency to approach things logically, methodically, and with prior planning.

The second phalange hints at the balance between the person's ideals or ambitions and the realization of his talents, and indicates the degree of practicality in the person's life. A long phalange (relative to the other phalanges) indicates positive balance and a large measure of practicality and logic; a short phalange reveals a large gap between ambition and implementation and a tendency to "dream" rather than to accomplish.

The third phalange teaches us about the person's physical desires, and mainly about the instincts which affect the person and the degree of violence in his character. A thick and large phalange indicates a love for physical desires and living for their satisfaction; a thin and small phalange shows a tough character, selfish and cruel; a phalange that is suitably formed in relation to the rest of the finger indicates a pleasant nature, generosity, and a balance between physical and spiritual desires.

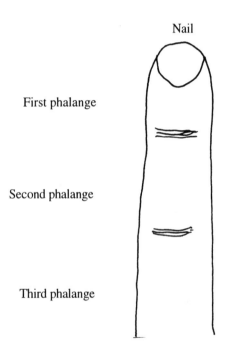

Nail

First phalange

Second phalange

Third phalange

The Joints of the Fingers

The palmist must pay special attention to the joints of the fingers. The accepted differentiation is smooth joints (which create a straight line with the finger) versus prominent joints (whose circumference is larger than the circumference of the finger).

Smooth joints indicate a tendency towards intuitive activity — activity that is based on emotion rather than thought. The smooth joints teach us, therefore, about the manner in which the person will act, but not the area in which he will act.

Prominent joints signify a tendency towards action which comes after thought and planning, and a preference for logic over emotion. People with prominent joints are precise and basic, paying attention to the minutiae in all areas of their life.

The joints of the fingers tell us about the way a person acts. Within a given sphere — let us say in medicine — a doctor with smooth joints will show a tendency towards intuitive diagnosis, while a doctor with prominent joints would prefer diagnosing only after collecting most of the necessary data.

The Fingernails and Health

The nails, as has been known for many years, can reveal diseases that are liable to plaçe a person at risk. In the past, those who dealt with healing know that certain marks on the nails hinted at particular illnesses. Today, we know that signs expressed in the nails — white or bluish stains, cracks, and the like — can indicate, among other things, improper nutrition and circulatory or metabolic problems in the body.

A palmist can use the fingernails to learn about a person's health (or health risks), but we must not forget that a person's character is also expressed in his fingernails — it is common knowledge that nail-biting indicates nervousness.

The basic differentiation is between long fingernails and short fingernails, and these are subdivided into broad or narrow fingernails.

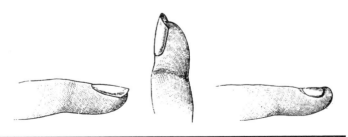

Weakness of the lungs.

General weakness of the
digestive system.

Medical problems with
bronchitis, the throat and
nose.

Medical problems in the
circulatory system and
the heart.

Danger of paralysis
or stroke.

Long Fingernails

Long fingernails indicate that the person suffers primarily from illnesses in the upper portion of his body — the head and chest.

Long, narrow fingernails indicate problems in the lungs and chest.

Fingernails that are long and broad suggest problems in the windpipe and the esophagus.

Long fingernails that are broad at the base and narrow at the top indicate circulatory problems, primarily in the veins. Occasionally, there may also be bluish stains under the nails (especially in women).

Very long and narrow fingernails indicate physical weakness and instability of the spinal cord.

White spots on long fingernails signify problems in the nervous system.

People with long fingernails tend to behave moderately, have an optimistic spirit, and love beautiful art even if they do not deal with this in actuality. They take everything seriously, but when reality contradicts their opinions or beliefs, they would prefer to avoid conflict rather than undermine their faith.

Short Fingernails

Short fingernails indicate that a person suffers primarily from heart problems and illnesses in the lower portion of his body.

Short and narrow nails indicate heart trouble and circulatory problems (it is important to check the crescent at the base of the nail — a large, prominent crescent indicates normal circulation; a small crescent shows abnormal circulation).

Short and broad nails indicate problems, even as serious as paralysis or stroke, in the nervous system.

People with short nails are active and have "both feet firmly planted on the ground." Their sense of logic is sharp and they are quick in both action and thought. They tend to stand up for themselves and to stubbornly strive towards the achievement of their objectives; they have a sense of humor.

Those with short, broad nails, in which the nail is wider than it is long, tend towards verbal violence and unnecessary arguments.

The Thumb

The thumb receives special treatment by the palmist — actually, it receives such special treatment that in the Far East, alongside the palm readers, there are thumb readers!

The thumb can teach us about a person's abilities and characteristics, no less than the different mounts or lines on the palm, and therefore, we give the thumb special attention. The special position of the thumb on the palm, opposite the fingers (and not alongside them) is the characteristic which differentiates between man and animal. If we compare a chimpanzee's thumb with a person's thumb, we can see that the person's thumb is longer, more free in its movements and is capable of reaching over as far as the base of the pinkie. There are those who claim that the longer and more flexible a person's thumb is, the higher their position on the ladder of intellectual development.

Research has shown that people who are mentally deficient have small, under-developed thumbs, and that people who are spiritually accomplished have large, well-developed thumbs.

After birth, an infant holds his thumb underneath his fingers, and as he develops, the baby "releases" his thumb from the protection of his fingers, enabling it to move about freely. During sleep, the thumb sometimes reverts back to the protection of the fingers. Following death, the hand is often in a position where the thumb has retreated back underneath the fingers, and the hand has closed into a fist.

From this we can learn that the position and free movement of the thumb in relation to the other fingers symbolizes, to a large extent, the mental development of a person — at birth the development is only just beginning, it is dormant during sleep, and ends at death.

The closer the thumb is located to the other fingers and the more its movements are limited to the movements of the other fingers, the lower the mental development of the person.

When the thumb is far from the index finger next to it, moves freely and extends at a straight angle from the palm, the person is at a high stage of mental development.

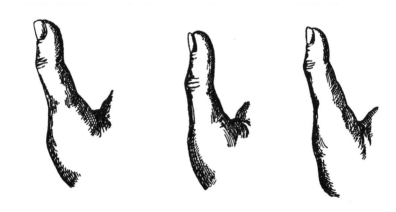

People who tend to make fists with their hands while they speak and to hide their thumbs under their fingers, are people who lack self-confidence.

A large, straight thumb which extends prominently from the hand indicates spiritual and mental ability.

A short, thick thumb which is close to the hand, indicates a person whose behavior is controlled by his desires and basic passions.

A long thumb with straight, pleasant lines signifies a person who has succeeded in fulfilling his aspirations and sees pleasure in his life.

A long thumb that forms more than a ninety degree angle with the index finger indicates an extreme nature and a tendency to be extraordinary.

A long thumb shows a tendency towards spiritual and mental activity.

A short thumb signifies a tendency towards physical activity.

A short, slender thumb shows a lack of willpower and mental weakness.

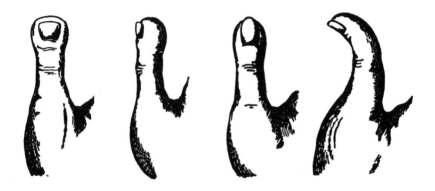

Once we have determined the type of thumb, we must continue to examine the parts of the thumb — the phalanges — and their relationship to each other.

The first phalange (with the fingernail). This phalange indicates the strength of a person's will and the energy that he can produce from within.

When this phalange is long (relative to the second phalange), this shows a stubborn person who tries to do everything in his own way; when the phalange is equal in length (to the second phalange), this signifies a person who carefully considers his actions; when the phalange is short (shorter than the second phalange), this indicates a weak-willed person.

The second phalange (in the middle). This explains the person's logic. A long phalange (relative to the first phalange) shows us that the person acts on the basis of logic and intellectual analysis, and not on the basis of spontaneous emotion.

If the second phalange is equal in length to the first phalange, this means the person acts wisely and uses his "common sense."

If the second phalange is shorter than the first phalange, this indicates a person who tends to act rashly, without thinking or considering the consequences.

The third phalange (which connects to the Mount of Venus). This indicates the effect that love and sexual desire has on a person's actions. The longer the phalange (relative to the whole thumb), the more that person — man or woman — tends to act on the basis of his sexual feelings or emotional relationships. If the thumb is long but this phalange is short, the person could lose his entire world because of love or sexual desire that controls him.

Now we shall examine **the flexibility of the thumb**. This flexibility is expressed mainly in the first joint. We distinguish between a flexible thumb, where the first phalange bends backwards and when pressed upon forms a sort of backwards arch; and a stiff thumb, where the first phalange extends straight out from the thumb or tends to bend forward, and does not bend backwards, even under pressure.

The flexible thumb indicates a flexible character, a person's sense of opportunism, a readiness to move from one situation to another, and an ability to "land on one's feet," no matter what the circumstances. The stiff thumb signifies conformity to a certain pattern of behavior and way of life, caution, and stubbornness. Faithfulness is a most prominent trait of those with a stiff thumb.

The musculature at the base of the thumb determines the changes in the line of life. In addition to the flexibility of the thumb, we must examine the muscles at the base of the thumb and see if they, too, are flexible or stiff.

The thumb is the most important finger, and therefore, it must be examined carefully and thoroughly. It is important to remember that in addition to examining the phalanges and the flexibility, you must check everything you look for in the other fingers: the shape; the fingernail; and the joints. It is best to examine the other fingers, and only then, to thoroughly examine the thumb.

THE MOUNTS OF THE HAND

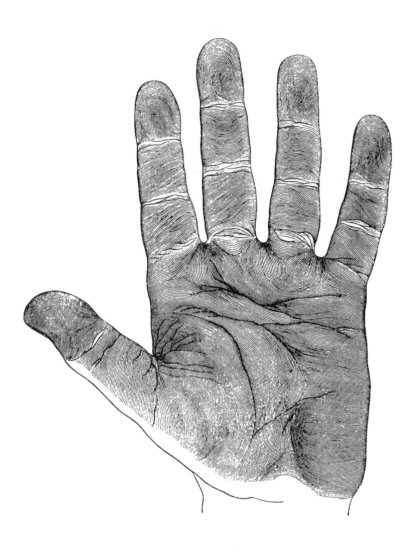

The Mounts of the Hand

The palm has seven mounts, each of them representing the influence of a particular planet on one's life and character. The strong bond between astrology and palmistry is not necessarily expressed in the names of the mounts found on the hand, but primarily in the relationship that exists between the dominant planets in a person's life (as can be learned from his horoscope) and the mounts which are most prominent and developed on the palm.

We will see, for example, that people whose birth was affected by a strong positive (ascending) influence from the planet Venus, will also have a prominent Mount of Venus on their palm; and if their horoscope tells of a strong negative (descending) influence at birth, the Mount of Venus will be flat. At this juncture we will not discuss all the reciprocal effects and connections between astrology and palmistry, but when describing each of the mounts, the corresponding dates of birth will be noted.

On the following page is a map showing the locations of the mounts of the palm and the names of each one. Notice that the names of the seven mounts (the lower Mount of Mars and the upper Mount of Mars, in actuality, two parts of a single mount that are separated) correspond to the names of the seven traditional astrological planets.

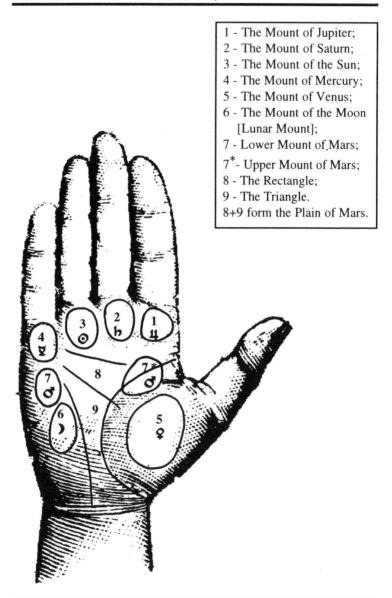

1 - The Mount of Jupiter;
2 - The Mount of Saturn;
3 - The Mount of the Sun;
4 - The Mount of Mercury;
5 - The Mount of Venus;
6 - The Mount of the Moon
    [Lunar Mount];
7 - Lower Mount of Mars;
7* - Upper Mount of Mars;
8 - The Rectangle;
9 - The Triangle.
8+9 form the Plain of Mars.

Some characteristics regarding all the mounts:

1. A mount which is well-developed and very prominent indicates a large proportion, even to the point of exaggeration, of the characteristic represented by that mount. Occasionally it can reach a situation where one mount, unusually developed, takes over and covers up another mount.

2. A developed mount that is not exaggerated indicates a perfect level of that particular characteristic.

3. An undeveloped mount shows there is a certain lack of that particular characteristic.

4. A flat mount signifies that the subject actually lacks that particular characteristic.

5. A hollow found where a mount should be means a hatred of the characteristic represented by the mount, and a tendency to act contrary to the way in which the mount would seem to indicate.

6. People with prominent, well-developed mounts tend towards sentimentality and emotional behavior, while people with flat mounts are more indifferent and act on the basis of logic.

It is clear that only the experience of the palmist can teach him to distinguish between the different degrees of each mount. In any event, the palmist must learn early on to differentiate between a developed, prominent and broad mount (which is considered to be positive) and a mount which is flat and narrow (considered to be negative.)

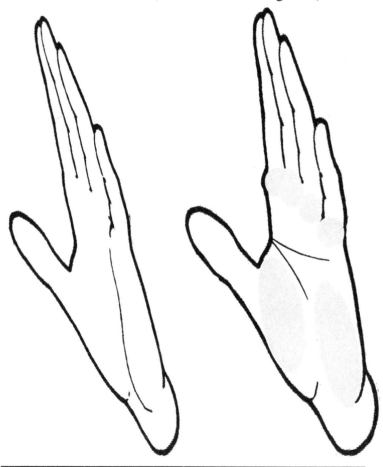

The Mount of the Moon

The Mount of the Moon, or the Lunar Mount, is located in the lower part of the palm below the Line of Head.

1. A developed Lunar Mount indicates a rich imagination, a tendency towards idealism, a talent for inventing and developing ideas. Such people enjoy innovation in all their activities, they are lovers of travel and enjoy making a variety of contacts with different people (born end of June to July).

2. A flat Lunar Mount indicates logic and intelligence, but no creativity. These types of people tend to lead structured lives, according to the rules of behavior that society dictates. For the most part they may tend towards religious extremism and activity in political parties (born end of January to February).

The Mount of Jupiter

The Mount of Jupiter is located at the base of the first finger (closest to the thumb).

1. A well-developed Mount of Jupiter shows an ambitious nature, self-confidence and a high degree of emotional energy. These types of people tend to be persevering, display initiative, and know how to motivate people. They try to do everything perfectly. Unfortunately, only a few of them succeed in fully achieving their ambitions (born end of November to December).

2. A flat Mount of Jupiter shows intellectual ability and a great deal of knowledge; people with good memories and the ability to understand. Their ambitions lie in the emotional and spiritual realm and are not expressed in physical action. For the most part, they utilize their talents in helping others succeed with their aspirations (born end of February to March).

The Mount of Venus

The Mount of Venus is located at the base of the thumb, beneath the Line of Life.

1. A prominent Mount of Venus signifies desire, love of beauty, a love of the arts; these types of people tend to give pleasure to others and deal in the arts. There is a considerable power of sexual attraction, which occasionally causes the person to act rashly due to his passions of the moment (born end of April to May).

2. A flattened Mount of Venus signifies a conflict between the love of beauty and passion, and cold reason. Such people tend to act logically, and sometimes their logic will prevent them from acting on the basis of their feelings. These people often work in fields requiring cold reasoning while they gaze longingly at other passion-filled realms (born end of September to October).

The Mount of Mercury

The Mount of Mercury is located at the base of the little finger.

1. A developed Mount of Mercury indicates instability, a two-faceted aspect in the subject's personality. These types of people are inconsistent and have difficulty connecting with their surroundings. They are successful in their business dealings. They can live in peace only with those people who accept and understand the instability in their nature (born end of May to June).

2. A flat Mount of Mercury indicates a harmonious, moral character; stability; and a tendency towards practical actions. Sometimes a materialistic nature becomes dominant and these people become miserly and introverted (born end of August to September).

The Mount of Saturn

The Mount of Saturn is located at the base of the second (middle) finger.

1. If the Mount of Saturn is prominent, this means the person possesses a strong will and intelligence, independent thought and generosity. These people tend to keep to their own private lives; they are often religious. Occasionally, they may lapse into melancholy and depression (born end of December to January).

2. A flat Mount of Saturn means the person has a strong will and intelligence, emotional sensitivity and honest friendships. These people like to be in public and spend time with their companions (born end of January to February).

3. If there is no Mount of Saturn, this shows extreme instability in all the person's activities.

The Mount of Mars

The Mount of Mars appears on the line which divides the hand into two semi-circles. If you fold your hand, you can see the Mount of Mars in the fold, beginning from the Line of Life (beneath it) and between the Line of Heart and the Line of Head (the Square of Mars). The Line of Life, therefore, divides the Mount of Mars into two mounts. [There are those who refer to them as the Upper Mount of Mars, on the right, and the Lower Mount of Mars on the left; alternatively, they are called the Mount of Mars and the Square Mount Mars.]

Lower Mount

Upper Mount

1. When the mount beneath the Line of Life is prominent and developed, this show courage, determination, and an uncompromising instinct to fight. These sorts of people love to be among their "fans" who agree with them all the time. In the event of a crisis, they are

likely to "break" easily and fall into depression, drinking, or drugs (born end of March to April). In most cases, when the Mount of Mars is pronounced, the second mount (the Square of Mars) is also pronounced.

2. When the Mount of Mars is flat (this will primarily be seen in the Square of Mars which is flat, almost a hollow), the person tends towards courageous speech rather than action, and uses deception and trickery to achieve his goals. These people change their minds often and their lives are a winding road (born end of October to November).

The Mount of the Sun

The Mount of the Sun is located at the base of the third finger (the ring finger near the little finger), and is also referred to as the Mount of Apollo, after the Greek god who loved beauty.

1. When the Mount of the Sun is developed, this shows a love of beauty, openness, and generosity. These people tend to deal in areas that bring them fame, wealth, and respect. They have principles and a solid nature, and are liked by people around them. At times of crisis, they may tend to "break" and sink into depression (born end of July to August).

2. A flat Mount of the Sun shows a love of accolade and a desire to be at the center. These people tend to deal in those fields where they can wield a great deal of influence, through an institution or their employer, rather than through their own talents. They are successful in business, but they do not achieve extraordinary wealth or success (born end of January to February).

THE LINES AND MARKS ON THE PALM

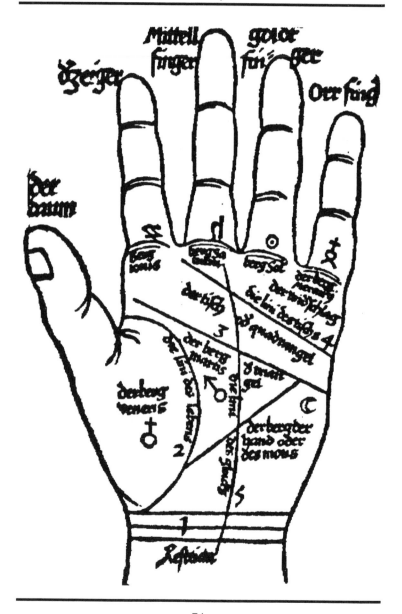

The Lines of the Palm

Now that we have reached the lines on the palm, we turn to the section which is more commonly known as Chiromancy.

Every line is significant, each mark and shading, every branch and twist, has meaning. It is not easy to read the lines on the palm, and when doing so, one must work carefully and cautiously.

Reading the lines of the palm should be done with the subject facing the palmist, with the palms lighted. Remember that the lines are read last, following the general impression, the fingers, and the mounts, when the palmist already knows something about the subject.

To see the lines properly, you can press with your thumb lightly on the palm and stretch the skin, so that the line becomes clearer.

Many palmists use a drawing of the palm on which they can indicate the lines and marks they find on the subject's palm. Later on, this can help the palmist draw his conclusions about the subject's character and future.

Before we look at the lines themselves, let's talk about the lines in general, the characteristics to look for with each line, and the marks found on the palm. Then, we can outline the importance of each detail on every line.

There are three major lines: The Line of Life, the Line of Heart, and the Line of Head. Four additional lines complete the first "group of seven" lines on the palm: the Line of Fate (Line of Saturn), the Line of the Sun, the Girdle of Venus, and the Line of Health.

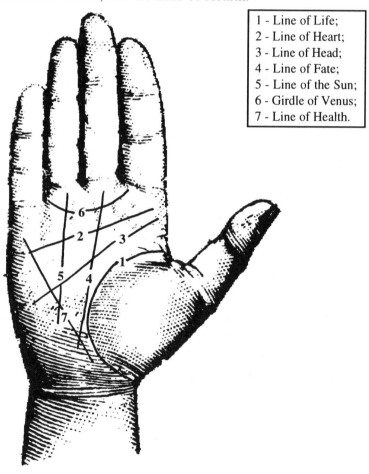

1 - Line of Life;
2 - Line of Heart;
3 - Line of Head;
4 - Line of Fate;
5 - Line of the Sun;
6 - Girdle of Venus;
7 - Line of Health.

Seven additional lines, of lesser importance, comprise the "second group of seven": Line of Mars, Line of Passion, Line of Intuition, Line of Marriage, the First Bracelet, the Second Bracelet, and the Third Bracelet (the bracelets are located at the wrist).

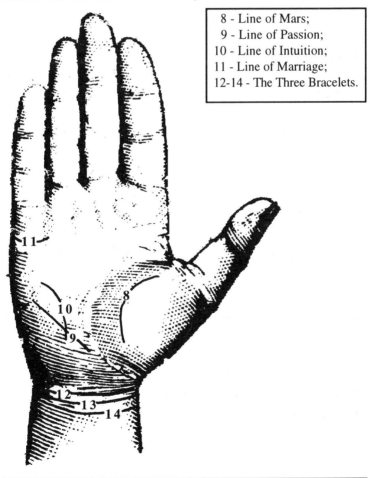

8 - Line of Mars;
9 - Line of Passion;
10 - Line of Intuition;
11 - Line of Marriage;
12-14 - The Three Bracelets.

The following is true for all the lines on the palm:

The more clearly and continuous the line appears, the greater its influence will be.

A pale line indicates a physical weakness and lack of energy.

A reddish line shows activity, energy, and optimism.

A yellowish line means digestive problems, pride, and selfishness.

A grayish line signifies indifference, arrogance, and a tendency towards depression.

We may find the following types of lines:

A twin line – A line which is found to parallel another line (usually one of the three major lines), and this reinforces the original line and sometimes it can also replaces it in times of crisis.

A branch at the end of a line –
When the line branches off into two
lines but not more, this strengthens
the line.

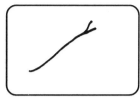

A "brush" at the end of the line –
When a line branches off into many
thin lines which continue in the
direction of the original line, this
weakens the effect of the line.

Offshoots – Short lines which
ascend or descend from the original
line, these strengthen the power of
the line when the ascend (towards
the fingers) and weaken the line with
they descend (towards the wrist).

"Chains" or "islands" on the line
indicate a weakness and instability
in the line.

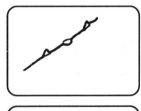

Breaks (gaps) in the line indicate a
serious crisis.

An example of a lucky palm:

1. A double Line of Life;
2. Line of Fate (Saturn) is straight, indicating abundant happiness;
3. Line of Heart is strengthened by lines branching off;
4. Love which is realized;
5. A prominent Girdle of Venus;
6. A complete Line of Head, clear and reinforced by lines branching off, indicates a multitude of talents;
7. Economic success in the field of arts;
8. Uniting of Mercury and Venus signifies an excellent between love and balance wealth;
9. Good health;
10. The bracelets indicate a long life;
11. A single great love.

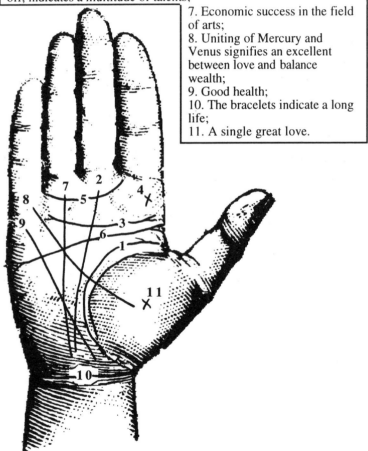

"Waves" weaken the effect of the line.

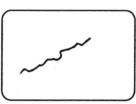

"Hairs" – Thin lines which parallel or continue the original line – weaken the effect of the line. Networks of "hairs" over the entire surface of the palm indicate an inconsistency which effects all the lines.

Dots on the line indicate difficulties and problems.

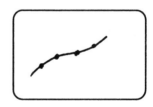

The Marks of the Palm

Now we must learn about several marks which appear on the palm (their meaning will be discussed later on).

Star – an important mark whose location on a mount or line determines its meaning. Usually indicates a positive development.

Square – a mark which usually warns of danger.

Dot – A mark which signifies a physical or mental illness.

Cross – A mark whose location on the palm determines its meaning. It usually indicates a negative change.

Grill – A mark found on the mounts which signifies difficulties in realizing the characteristic represented by that mount.

Stripes – This mark strengthens the characteristic which is expressed by the particular mound where the stripes are found (a similar effect to that of offshoots which ascend from the line).

Island – a negative mark regarding the line on which it is found (a continuous line of islands creates a "chain").

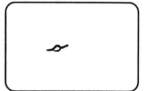

Circle – a negative mark (usually), it is quite rare.

Triangle – a positive mark, it sometimes appears in the shape of an arrow, and this also has a positive influence.

The Line of Life

The Line of Life borders the Mount of Venus, at the base of the thumb, and teaches us about health (or illness and death) and about the solidity or weakness of a person's character. We can determine times on the Line of Life, in other words, when a particular event took place or will take place (see the chapter on Determining Time).

A long, continuous Line of Life, free of breaks, intersections or stars, uniform in color along its entire length and clearly visible, indicates a long, healthy life and a solid character.

A short Line of Life (particularly if the line is identical on both hands) indicates a short life. However, if there is a twin line, or the Line of Mars, which continues and passes the Line of Life towards the wrist, the twin line or the Line of Mars takes the place of the Line of Life and the life of the subject will continue beyond the point of time where it stopped.

If the Line of Life is broken on one palm but complete on the other palm (most often it will be broken on the left hand and complete on the right hand), this signifies a serious illness from which the subject can be cured. The location of the break indicates the age at which the person will fall ill.

If the Line of Life is composed of chains (circles or islands), or is made up of many tiny line fragments, this indicates ill health. If the line continues as a chain along its entire length, this indicates ill health throughout the person's life. If only part of the line is broken, this will tell us which period during his life the person suffered or will suffer from ill health.

A broad, flat Line of Life means a rude and violent nature.

A narrow Line of Life signifies a melancholy nature.

If the Line of life has a bluish or grayish hue, this indicates a chronic illness which will appear at the age where the line changes its color to bluish or grayish.

A cross on the Line of Life indicates an isolated event which will have a major effect on the subject.

If the Line of Life curls up at its end into a half-circle (usually at the bottom, under the Mount of Venus), this indicates a long life and good health.

All the lines which parallel the Line of Life, if they are complete and continuous, signify a positive influence and can undo any damage found in the Line of Life.

All the lines which cross the Line of Life indicate negative influences and disturbances and pressures in the subject's life. If one of the intersecting lines is broken, or it has an island or other negative mark on it, this increases the negative effect.

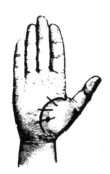

The Line of Health is very important in the event that the Line of Life is broken, short, or resembles a chain. A deep and continuous Line of Health can replace the Line of Life and repair the damage it contains (just like a twin line or the Line of Mars).

A long and continuous Line of Life, accompanied by a twin line (or the Line of Mars), in addition to a long and continuous Line of Health, indicates excellent health, a strong character, and success in all areas of life.

The space between the Line of Life and the Line of Head (relative to the width of the hand) determines the intelligence, logic, and intellect in a person's life. If the space is too narrow (1), this signifies a small amount of intelligence, while too large (3) a space indicates a degree of rashness and lack of intelligence in the person's life. A moderate amount (2) of space between the two lines means a proper and successful balance between intelligence and independent thought and action, and it is a good sign in the person's life.

If the Line of Life, the Line of Head, and the Line of Heart are connected at their source, this indicates sudden death from an accident or violent action, but there is no way of knowing at what age this will occur. The person with a connected line has a tendency towards acting rashly, unnecessary personal risk, and "getting into trouble" wherever he turns.

Branches that are "smooth" and pleasant-looking as they come off the Line of Life, particularly if they are ascending upwards (towards the fingers) mean success at the point in life at which the branch appears.

A branch which goes from the Line of Life towards he Mount of Jupiter indicates an ambitious nature, and that the person strives towards material success.

A branch which goes from the Line of Life towards the Mount of Venus signifies an adventurous, sensual nature, with a tendency towards travel and change in one's personal life. (The degree to which the subject will realize this tendency depends on the shape of the hand.)

Small lines ("hairs") which appear
on the side of the Line of Life will
weaken it.

An intersecting line which goes
from the Mount of Venus, crosses
the Line of Life and reaches the
Square of Mars, indicates a nervous
disorder at the point where the
intersecting line crosses the Line of
Life.

An intersecting line which goes
from the Mount of Venus, crosses
the Line of Life, and disappears in
the middle of the hand means the
person suffers from emotional
problems and stress.

A line which crosses the Line of
Life and reaches the Line of
Marriage signifies a divorce or
another crisis in the subject's family
life.

A line which crosses the Line of
Life as well as the Line of the Sun
indicates a serious crisis in the
person's social status.

A line which crosses the Line of
Life and also crosses the Line of
Fate signifies a serious crisis
relating to property and business.

A faint Line of Life indicates health problems with a person's respiratory system.

If the Line of Life is broken, with a square appearing at the place where it breaks, this means that the person will be saved from an illness (or from death). The square indicates that the subject will overcome the crisis and will recover.

An island on the Line of Life signifies an illness, although if the Line of Life passes around the island, the subject will be saved from the illness.

A dot on the Line of Life indicates illness or injury.

The Line of Life is the most important line on the hand and any mark, every curve and line which touches the Line of Life is very significant. Therefore, the Line of Life should be examined carefully and cautiously, along its entire length, and its relationship to the other lines on the hand should be studied.

As we have said, it is possible to determine the subject's age using the Line of Life, and the time at which a particular event has occurred or will occur. Remember to determine the times using the Line of Life, and you will then be able to predict the future with great success. (See also the chapter on Determining Age.)

The Line of Head

The Line of Head begins between the thumb and the first finger (pointer) and continues across the palm. This line divides the palm into two halves. The upper half, with the fingers and the Mounts of Jupiter, Saturn, Sun, Mercury, and Mars, represents the intellect and consciousness. The lower half—the base of the hand, the thumb, the Mount of Venus, and the Lunar Mount— represents the body and the material. The Line of Head is sometimes referred to as the Line of Intellect.

The Line of Head teaches us about the subject's intellect, his abilities relating to thought and study, and his tendency to utilize his intellectual talents.

The Line of Head can begin in one of three different places:

1. From the top of the Line of Life (when it merges with the Line of Life at its start), which indicates hesitancy and a great deal of sensitivity. In many hands, the Line of Head begins here. Sometimes, the line itself doesn't merge with

the Line of Life, but rather is
connected to it by clear, deep
connecting lines.

2. From the Mount of Mars, it
touches the Line of Life and
continues towards the palm,
signifying nervousness, instability,
and a person who is easily angered.
(This kind of Line of Head is
also partially attached to the Line
of Life.)

3. From the Mount of Jupiter. In
rare cases, the Line of Head will
reach the Line of Life, and this
indicates energy and realized
ability, but most of the time this
type of line is characterized by the
fact that it does not connect to the
Line of Life.

If the Line of Head is disconnected from the Line of Life, this shows exaggerated self-confidence and a tendency towards making decisions rashly and intuitively, on the basis of emotion rather than logic. A person with this type of line must teach himself how to control his decisions and carefully consider the steps he takes. Usually, people with this type of disconnected Line of Head are successful early in their lives, but there is always the risk that their successes will collapse as a result of a single impulsive decision.

If the Line of Head is straight (that is, parallel to the wrist), and continuous, this indicates straightforward intelligence, sharp logic and a tendency towards using his intellect in the material world.

A Line of Head which is diagonal and continuous means the person has intellect, logic, and a tendency to act in the spiritual realm.

If the Line of Head is long, so that it reaches the edge of the palm (opposite the thumb), this shows that the subject concentrates on himself, and is egotistical.

A short Line of Head which crosses the Line of Fate and continues only a short distance past it, indicates that the person prefers the material to the intellectual, the body to the spirit.

A Line of Head consisting of a chain indicates a tendency towards inconsistency.

If the Line of Head and the Line of Heart are close together, and the Line of Head appears to be deeper and clearer than the Line of Heart, this means that the intellect will control the heart (and vice versa— if the Line of Heart is deeper and clearer than the Line of Head, the heart will control the intellect).

If the Line of Head has branches which go towards one of the mounts, this means the subject will tend to occupy himself (intellectually) with the realm represented by the mount.

If the Line of Head has a secondary line, this signifies that the person can excel in many areas that vary from each other.

A broken Line of Head (primarily if it is broken on both hands) indicates a mental disability.

An island weakens the Line of Head; a star strengthens the line; a square means the person will overcome problems and difficulties related to the Line of Head.

If the Line of Head is slanted
(downwards) and lies close to the
Line of Life, this indicates a lack of
self-confidence.

Remember that the Line of Head indicates a particular
direction in the nature and the life of the subject. However,
the practical expression of that direction is also affected by
the shape of the subject's hand and the shape of the mounts
on his hand.

(For example: A straight and horizontal Line of Head
on a square-shaped hand will strengthen the person's
tendency towards rational behavior and acting methodically
and thoroughly; but a slanted Line of Head on a square-
shaped hand will not be fully realized, and the person will
not necessarily deal in the arts or the spiritual realm.)

The Line of Heart

The Line of Heart goes across the hand, above the Line of Head, and beneath the mounts of the fingers. The Line of Heart is considered to be one of the major lines on a person's palm, since it teaches us about the person's attitudes and character in the area of love and sex—two very important spheres in a person's life.

The Line of Heart is a relatively long line, but it does not cross the entire hand. The line is clearly defined on the palm, but is not overly deep. The line usually has branches towards the mounts of the fingers.

A Line of Heart which is long and straight and goes across the hand almost entirely indicates a tendency towards mental cruelty, emotional violence, and jealousy which can lead to physical violence.

If the Line of Heart is close to the Line of Head, this signifies hypocrisy and deception in the person's character.

If the Line of Heart branches off towards the Mount of Jupiter, this shows that the subject is endowed with a great capacity for love and sensitivity.

If the Line of Heart is broken underneath the Mount of Saturn, this indicates a deep crisis in the subject's love relationships.

If the Line of Heart consists of a chain, or is composed of small line fragments, this signifies instability in the subject's love life.

If the Line of Heart is short and has a reddish hue, this indicates a strong love and physical desire.

If the Line of Heart is cut by short perpendicular lines, this shows a multitude of short, passing relationships.

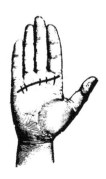

If the Line of Heart is close to the
Line of Head, and appears deeper
and clearer than the Line of Head,
this shows that the emotions of the
subject's heart will control the logic
of his intellect.

A yellowish long Line of Heart
indicates a person a suffers from
digestive disorders, which is
causing him to be nervous and
impatient.

Any breaks found on the Line of
Heart signify a crisis in the
person's love life; this is also true if
there is a dot found on the line.

If the Line of Heart is straight, with no branches or offshoots, this shows a person who is cool and calculating in all his actions.

If the Line of Heart has branches and offshoots, this indicates a sensitivity towards the love of others.

If the Line of Heart is short and blurred, so that it is difficult to distinguish, this signifies a person who is emotionally incapable of feeling love.

The Line of Fate

The Line of Fate is the line which ascends from the bracelets up towards the middle finger (the Finger of Saturn), and it is the line which vertically divides the hand into two halves. Remember that time is defined by the Line of Fate, and proceeds from bottom towards the top. The Line of Fate indicates the success or failure of a person in his material life.

In actuality, the Line of Fate provides the same data as the Line of Life, but in less detail; we can read the Line of Fate to help us confirm what we have already learned from the Line of Life.

A straight Line of Fate, clearly defined and continuous, is a good sign of the person's success.

If the Line of Fate curves towards a mount (and primarily if it veers off its straight path towards the Mount of San) this indicates the subject's success in the area signified by the mount towards which the line curves.

If the Line of Fate is stopped by the Line of Heart, this signifies that the person will encounter serious difficulties in realizing his ambitions.

If the Line of Fate is stopped by the Line of Head, this means that the person's mistakes will halt his success.

If the Line of Fate is cut off or full of breaks, this indicates that the subject will move from success to failure and vice versa, many times in his lifetime.

A double Line of Fate means success in many different areas.

A square on the Line of Fate reinforces the person's material success; an island or cross are bad signs, just like a break.

The Line of Fate is missing from the hand of people whose fate is determined by things around them, rather than by their own actions.

The Line of the Sun

The Line of the Sun (the Line of Apollo) indicates success or lack of success; in this sense it is similar to the Line of Fate, only it is more complicated to understand. The line begins under the Finger of the Sun and continues downward towards the wrist.

The main area about which the Line of the Sun can give an indication stems from the results of a person's abilities (and primarily in the area of the arts). The more clearly the line appears, the greater the success the person will have. The area in which the person will be successful is determined by the mounts which control the subject's hand.

Occasionally, we may see several parallel Lines of Sun, and this means that the person will deal in several areas, but a single Line of Sun indicates great success in a particular sphere. The Line of the Sun will appear on the hands of

those people who are successful in their area of choice.

A star appearing in the Line of the Sun strengthens the subject's success.

A square on the Line of the Sun is a reinforcing mark, and protects against obstacles.

An island on the Line of the Sun indicates difficulties.

A cross on the Line of the Sun
means signifies difficulty and even
a serious crisis.

Sometimes, no Line of the Sun appears on the person's hand, and this means that the subject (despite talents he might have) does not receive the fame and recognition he deserves for his abilities.

The Girdle of Venus

The Girdle of Venus is a semi-circle located beneath the second (middle) finger. The line begins between the first and second fingers (between the Mount of Jupiter and the Mount of Saturn), and goes around beneath the Mount of Saturn and the Mount of the Sun, ending between the third and fourth fingers (between the Mount of the Sun and the Mount of Mercury).

A clear Girdle of Venus tells about a person's sensuality; people with a pronounced Girdle of Venus are capable of becoming excited by and addicted to certain things. They move from one mood to another quickly.

If the Girdle of Venus continues towards the Line of Marriage, this tells us about difficulties in marriage due to mood swings.

A clear Girdle of Venus, a pronounced Mount of Venus and a long Line of Head indicate (particularly in women) a person who employs the power of desire on their partner for the purpose of control.

The Ring of Saturn

The Ring of Saturn appears on rare occasions as a line around the Mount of Saturn, beneath the second (middle) finger. The line indicates a person who does not succeed in realizing his ambitions and talents, and this is a bad sign on a person's hand. (The Ring of Saturn is not included among the 14 Lines of the Hand.)

The Line of Mars

The Line of Mars begins between
the thumb and the first finger, close
to the Mount of Mars, and goes
around the Mount of Venus in a
half-circle. Actually, the line
overlaps the Line of Life as it goes
around, but is inside, closer to the
Mount of Venus.

The Line of Mars, when it is clearly
outlined, long and complete,
strengthens the Line of Life – even
if the Line of Life is full of
fragments, for example, the person
will overcome the dangers and
crises.

If the Line of Mars is blurred and
broken, it cannot replace or fix, the
course of the Line of Life.

When the Line of Life and the Line of Mars are close to each other, and sometimes touch each other, this means that the person's life will be full of friction and arguments.

If the Line of Mars turns towards the center of the palm, either all of it or an offshoot from it, and crosses the Line of Life, this means there is impatience and egotism in the person's character.

The Line of Mars, in reality, is the line which accompanies the Line of Life, and because the Line of Life is so important, the Line of Mars is more important than any other ordinary accompanying line.

The Line of Health

The Line of Health begins near or on the Mount of Mercury, at the base of the little finger, and continues downward crossing the Line of the Sun, the Line of Head, and the Line of Fate, and ends near or at the end of the Line of Life. The Line of Health is also called Hepatica, or the Line of the Liver.

If the Line of Health is blurred (or totally absent), this signifies good physical health and a tendency to overcome pain and illness. (Indeed, it is the absence of the Line of Health on the palm which indicates good health!)

If the Line of Health is grayish or yellowish in color, this means problems with liver function.

If the Line of Health is reddish in color, this indicates physical immunity, together with a tendency towards heart disease.

If the Line of Health touches the Line of Life, this shows an illness or health problem at the point in time where the two lines intersect.

If the Line of Health is clear and straight along its entire length, this indicates that the person's digestive system is functioning properly.

If the Line of Health is winding and cut off, this means the person suffers from digestive problems.

If the Line of health crosses the
Line of Life, this signifies heart
disease.

If the Line of Health descends
vertically from the Mount of
Mercury, this indicates that the
subject's health problems will be
minimal.

If the Line of Health crosses the
hand horizontally, this shows that
the person's health problems will be
serious.

The Line of Passion

The Line of Passion is the line which touches or borders the Lunar Mount on the interior side (close to the center of the hand). Most often it begins above the bracelets and ascends diagonally upward towards the Finger of Mercury.

The path of this line is similar to that of the Line of Health, but we must not confuse the two.

A clear, long Line of Passion indicates that a person enjoys his life and his strong passions, which are expressed and realized.

If the Line of Passion continues across the hand parallel to the bracelets, cuts the Line of Life and ends at the Mount of Venus, this indicates that the person is addicted to his passions.

The Ring of Solomon

The Ring of Solomon is a ring which goes around the Mount of Jupiter. It appears rarely, and indicates that the person tends to believe in the mystical, the supernatural, and supernatural powers.

The Line of Intuition

The Line of Intuition appears on the hand on rare occasions, and when it does it appears as a half circle which begins at the Mount of Mercury and ends at the Lunar Mount. This line indicates that the person has a sensitive soul, with a tendency towards fantasies and imagination, and is influenced by things around him, sometimes to the point where he loses all sense of reality. (This is particularly true when the Line of Intuition appears on a spiritual or philosophical hand.)

The Line of Marriage

The Line of Marriage is the line which crosses the Mount of Mercury. The line is called the Line of Marriage, despite the fact that it tells us about friendship and love between people, and not necessarily about marriage. Because of the connection between love and marriage, it has been called the Line of Marriage, but the shape and direction of the line also affects the person's relationship with people close to him, including those of his own sex.

A long line signifies a long and stable marriage or love relationship.

A short line indicates a short and indecisive marriage or love relationship.

If the Line of Marriage crosses the Mount of Mercury in a clear, straight line without any marks or breaks, this means a long happy marriage, without any crises.

If the Line of marriage curls upward towards the fingers, this means the person is incapable of initiating a stable love relationship.

An island or a break on the Line of Marriage signifies a crisis or a break-up in a relationship; also, if the line points downward (across the palm) and branches off at the end, there is the danger of a serious crisis.

The Bracelets

We can distinguish the Bracelets—lines on the wrist beneath the palm—when we bend the hand over towards the arm. Sometimes there is a single bracelet which appears clearly, and sometimes we can see two of them, or even three bracelets.

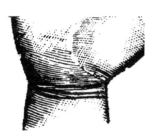

In the past, palmists counted each bracelet as one generation (that is, 30 years), and the more clearly the bracelet appeared the greater the degree of health and success with which the subject was endowed. A person with three clear bracelets could, in their opinion, expect a long, happy, and successful life.

Now palmists tend to believe that clearly defined bracelets indicate good health and blurred or indistinct bracelets indicate poor health, but they do not lend great deal of importance to the bracelets when reading the subject's palm.

If a cross appears on one of the bracelets, this indicates an inheritance the person will receive. If it appears on the first bracelet (close to the palm) this will happen in youth; if it appears on the second bracelet, in adulthood, and on the third bracelet, in old age.

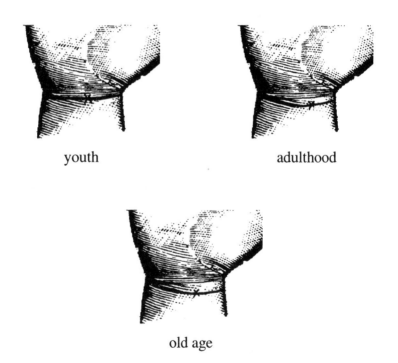

youth   adulthood

old age

Star

A star symbolizes an event which is beyond the control of the person's free will, although the results of that event can be changed by the power of the person's will. The star will usually appear when it is located on a mount or a line, and its meaning is determined by its location. When the star does not appear on a mount or a line, it will usually signify an illness or physical weakness. But a star on a mount or a line may be a good sign, and a symbol of luck.

A star on the Mount of Jupiter indicates success, respect, and fame that the person will receive. The higher up on the mount the star appears, the more successful he will be. We can also predict that the person—man or woman—will marry someone with a higher social status than their own.

A star on the Mount of Saturn is a **threatening symbol**, telling us of sudden death or serious illness. A star which is clearly visible is a sign of a violent injury. The farther away the star appears from the center of the mount, the less influence it will wield.

It is important to remember that a star that appears on the Finger of Saturn (middle) is a good sign and indicates unexpected success for the person. This type of star appeared, for example, on Napoleon's finger.

A star on the Mount of the Sun indicates material success, but also signifies a gap between the person's ambition and his achievement, which will lead to frustration and bitterness. We may assume that the person will succeed in his actions, but will not be happy. The person will be very famous.

A star on the Mount of Mercury shows that the person can expect success in the intellectual sphere—scientific research, writing, and thinking.

A star on the Mount of Mars indicates that the person will win fame and will be celebrated as an expert in his field.

A star on the Lunar Mount means that the subject will be hurt during his life in some way connected with water. The person may be successful due to his activities in the area of the arts, but he might also encounter disappointment and suffer from depression and feelings of frustration.

A star on the Mount of Venus indicates a person's success in his friendships and love relationships. The closer to the center of the mount the star appears, the more successful the person will be. If the star appears on the edge of the mount, this means that the person will be immersed in love, but will not always receive the same kind of love from his partner.

A star on the first phalange of the thumb means that the person will use the power of his will to overcome obstacles in his path.

A star on the second phalange of the thumb indicates that the person will suffer because of his partner's actions.

A star appearing on the first phalange of the fingers is a sign of good luck.

Grill

A grill is a sign that often appears on the mounts of the hand, and indicates either a weakening of the properties represented by the mount, or obstacles on the way to fulfilling those properties. That is, the effect of the grill depends on where it appears.

If it appears on the Mount of Jupiter, there are obstacles on the path to achieving the person's anticipated success.

If the grill appears on the Mount of Saturn, trouble awaits the person.

If it appears on the Mount of the Sun, there is a tendency to chase after empty things, which will make it difficult for the person to realize his talents.

On the Mount of Mercury, the grill indicates a fickleness that will make the person's life difficult.

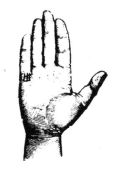

On the Lunar Mount, it indicates the person's constant, internal drive towards new things. In such a case, the grill can bring the person additional success... or failure in the sphere he has chosen to pursue.

If the grill is found on the Mount of Venus, it signifies a desire for the exotic and a chasing after dangerous pleasures.

Cross

In general, we can say that the cross is the opposite of the star—something which is beyond the subject's control and usually symbolizes bad luck and disaster. The significance of the cross is determined by its location on the palm.

A cross on the Mount of Jupiter indicates a great love in the person's life and, in most cases, this love will not lead to disaster in the person's life.

A cross on the Mount of Saturn testifies to a harmful accident.

A cross on the Mount of the Sun signifies a crisis in the material sphere.

A cross on the Mount of Mercury indicates that the person will get into trouble because of his tendency to lie.

A cross on the Mount of Mars means trouble for the person relating in the way of physical violence.

A cross on the Lunar Mount signifies a person whose imagination keeps him from reality.

A cross on the Mount of Venus indicates arguments and conflict in his love life or family life.

A cross on the Line of Head signifies physical injury which will harm his intellectual ability.

A cross on the Line of the Sun indicates that the person will lose his status in life as a result of a crime he himself has committed.

A cross on the Line of Heart indicates the death of someone upon whom the person depends.

Square

The square is a good sign, which indicates that the subject will succeed in overcoming an obstacle, crisis, or disaster written on the person's palm. If, for example, there is a break in the Line of Life (which indicates death or serious illness), and near the site of the break there is a square, this means that the person will overcome the danger of that death or illness. The square, therefore, is also referred to as "the shield," because it is a mark which shields the person from the negative effects of other marks.

The square can appear on either the lines or the mounts:

A square on a line, and primarily when the line crosses through the square and continues onward, indicates that the person will overcome an obstacle or disaster which appears on the line.

A square on a mount signifies that the person will not be hurt because of extremism regarding the characteristic represented by the mount. (For example, a square on the Mount of Mars means that the person will not be harmed by violence; a square on the Lunar Mount means that the person will not be hurt because of the influence of his imagination; a square on the Mount of Venus means the person will not be hurt because of a strong love, etc.).

Mount of Mars   Mount of Venus   Lunar Mount

Triangle or Arrow

The triangle or arrow appears clearly, usually on the mounts of the hand. It is a sign of success in the area represented by the mount upon which it appears.

When the triangle or arrow appears on a line, or close to a line, it indicates a tendency towards mystery and the person's desire to investigate things beyond their obvious appearance.

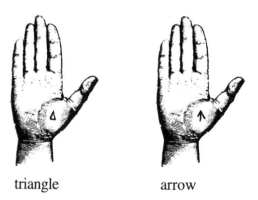

triangle   arrow

Island

The island is a mark indicating a disability or weakness on that particular place where the island appears. An island on the Line of Life, for example, indicates an illness, while an island on the Line of Head indicates a mental disability. However, the effect of the island is limited in its duration and its strength.

For the most part, an island indicates a weakness which the person will overcome, and sometimes the island's effect on the person will not even be felt.

There is a difference between an island that appears on a line and an island that appears on a mount:

If the island appears on a line, this signifies a short-term weakness or disability in that sphere represented by the line.

If the island appears on a mount, this indicates a weakness (over time) of the mount's positive aspect. (An island on the Mount of Mars, for example, indicates cowardice; an island on the Lunar Mount indicates a weak imagination, etc.).

Dot

The dot is a symbol of a short-term illness. The part of the person's body which will be affected is determined in two ways:

1. By the location of the dot. Experience will teach the palmist to distinguish these locations.

2. By the color of the dot: a red dot indicates damage to the head; a dark dot indicates damage to the nerves; a bright dot indicates an illness relating to high fever.

Circle

In general, the circle indicates a bad sign relating to its location. The circle usually appears on mounts and signifies crisis or harm relating to the characteristic represented by the mount.

(There are those who claim that a circle on the Mount of the Sun is a good sign, but there are many who differ with this statement.)

circle on the Mount of the Sun

Bands

Bands on the palm appear as thin lines, close to one another, and they appear on the fingers and the mounts of the hand. Most of the time, the direction of these lines is along the length of the hand (from the fingers towards the wrist).

Vertical bands on the fingers strengthen the properties of the mounts that are connected to each of the fingers and are an indication of the power the person has in a particular area—the more bands there are the greater the power.

Horizontal bands on the fingers weaken the properties of the mounts.

Vertical bands from the Line of Life to the fingers strengthen the Line of Life.

When there are lines on the mounts of the hand, we must distinguish between vertical lines, which strengthen the property of that mount, and horizontal lines, which weaken the property of the mount.

Vertical   Horizontal

The Great Quadrangle

The Great Quadrangle is the area which lies between the Line of Head and the Line of Heart.

When it resembles a broad rectangle, and the skin is smooth and taut, this indicates a stable nature and a balance between the person's intellect and emotions.

When the quadrangle resembles a narrow rectangle, this indicates that the person has narrow horizons.

When the quadrangle resembles a very wide rectangle, the person will display a tendency towards extremism in his relations with those around him.

If the quadrangle is wide at its sides and narrow in the middle, this means a lack of self-confidence and a tendency towards egotism.

If the Great Quadrangle creates a cone-shaped figure, this means that person tends to change his mind and his perspective, goes from being closed-minded to open (or vice-versa), and is greatly affected by his environment.

A quadrangle which is free from little lines indicates a tendency towards a quiet, stable life.

A quadrangle which is marked with little lines indicates a tendency towards nervousness and uncertainty.

A star appearing within the Great Quadrangle is a positive sign and signifies that the person is assured success.

The Great Triangle

The Great Triangle, which is sometimes referred to as the Triangle of Mars, is the triangle created by the Line of Life, the Line of Head, and the Line of Health. Sometimes the Line of Health is missing and then the Line of the Sun forms the third line of the Triangle. Such a triangle usually indicates success.

If the Great Triangle is clearly visible and includes within it the Square of Mars, this signifies an open and free way of thinking and a tendency to work for the general good.

If the Triangle is small and indistinct, this indicates hesitancy, deviousness, and a certain tendency to be subservient to dominant people.

The Triangle contains three angles. Each of them should be examined individually.

1. **The upper angle—**
between the Line of Head and the
Line of Life:

An acute angle indicates sharp logic
and sensitivity towards others.

An obtuse angle indicates
materialism and insensitivity to the
feelings of others.

An obtuse angle with very long
sides shows a tendency to hurt and
harm others.

2. **The side angle—**

between the Line of Head and the
Line of Health:

An acute angle signifies an ability
to learn quickly, a love of life, and
good health.

An obtuse angle signifies a steady
and stable life.

3. **The lower angle**—between the Line of Life and the Line of Health or the Line of the Sun:

When the angle is formed by the Line of Life and the Line of Health, an acute angle communicates a tendency towards low esteem and indecision, while an obtuse angle indicates a determination in the person's decisions.

When the angle is formed by the Line of Life and the Line of the Sun, an acute angle indicates a drive towards self-realization, and an obtuse angle signifies an openness to new ideas and a readiness to accept the opinions of others.

APPENDICES:

Determining Age

We can use the lines on the hand to determine when a particular event has occurred, or will occur. The subject's age can be determined only by using the lines. The closer the event (indicated by a star, island, etc.) appears to the beginning of the line, the better we can assume that it is related to an early age; and the closer the sign appears to the end of the line, the older the subject will be when the event takes place.

There are several methods for dividing the Line of Life according to age:

1. Some palmists take a sample of the Line of Life and divide it into equal portions, defining one end of the line as the first year of life and the other end of the line as old age. The subject's Line of Life is compared to the sample, and it can then be divided according to age.

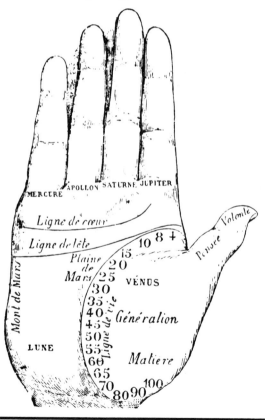

2. Another means for dividing the line according to age is based on finding two points along the subject's Line of Life: the point indicating age 35 and the point indicating age 49. These two numbers are related to the number 7 (5 x 7 and 7 x 7), which is very significant in predicting the future. This division is performed in several stages:

a. A line is drawn between the intersection point of the Line of Head and the Line of Fate, and between a point in the center of the Mount of Mercury (beneath the little finger). Continue this line until it crosses the line of life; this is the point of age 35.

b. A line is drawn from the lower end of the Line of Head to the center of the Mount of Venus. The point at which this line crosses the Line of Life is the point of age 49.

c. The Line of Life is now divided according to the ratio between these two points.

(According to this method, the intersection point between the Line of Fate and the Line of Head is also age 35 on the Line of Fate, and this line can also be divided according to age, with the younger ages being closer to the wrist, and the older ages being closer to the base of the fingers. See following page.)

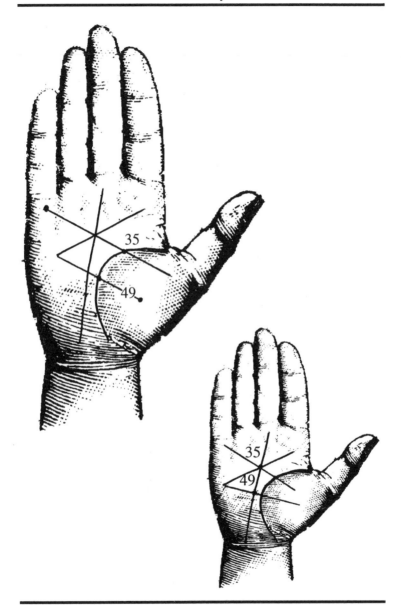

3. A different method for dividing the Line of Life according to age is based on lines that are drawn between the point in the center of the Mount of Venus and points between the fingers. The first line is drawn towards the beginning of the Line of Life. The second line is drawn to the point between the first and second fingers, and so forth. The last line is drawn to the point on the outside of the little finger (which will be similar to the line drawn in the first step of the second method).

These five lines give us five points on the Line of Life. Point 1 is birth; Point 2 is age 14; Point 3 is age 21; Point 4 is age 28; and Point 5 is age 35.

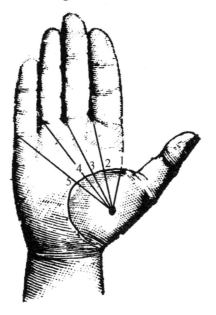

We now divide the remainder of the line according to the ratios we obtained, remembering that the segments (with each one, except for the first, representing 7 years), will in most cases be of different lengths, and that complex calculations are required in order to obtain the proper ratio for continuing to divide the Line of Life.

These three different methods will lead to the same result. In general, only professional palmists can read the subject's age accurately and an amateur is best off being satisfied with a general idea regarding the range of the subject's age. The best method is to divide the Line of Life into four parts: childhood, adolescence, maturity, and old age (instead of trying to predict the precise age at which a particular event occurred or will occur).

Palm Prints

A palmist can take a subject's palm print and read the lines and mounts that are found on the palm (making it possible to read a person's palm even if he is far away, or the palm of someone who has died, through reading an impression of his palm print). There are three methods for doing this:

1. For the purpose of taking the palm print, several tools are needed:
   a. Printing ink—black ink from a print shop, which should be diluted before being used.
   b. A small roller or small ink pad in order to rub the ink in an even layer on the subject's hand.
   c. Porous paper (thin cardboard, for example, with a matte, rather than a glossy finish).
   d. A piece of rubber or foam, approximately 1 cm. thick.

Place the paper on the piece of rubber. Spread the ink on the roller and rub it thoroughly over the subject's palm, pressing the back of the hand towards the roller so that even the depressions in the palm are covered with ink. Set down the roller and place the palm on the paper in one single motion (without moving it to the right or the left). Press down on the back of the hand. Lift up the hand in one single motion, making sure that the paper does not stick to the hand.

The ink can be removed with soap or special powder.

Allow the impression to dry well before beginning to examine it. (Impressions that you want to preserve for a long time should be covered with shellac, which can be purchased in spray form and keeps the color from becoming blurred).

2. An impression can also be obtained by placing the hand on the surface of a photocopier and copying it at different exposures until a suitable result is obtained.

3. It is also possible to take a photograph of the subject's palm using a regular or Polaroid camera.